THE THIN BOOK OF®

NAMING
ELEPHANTS

*How to Surface Undiscussables
for Greater Organizational Success*

*Sue Annis Hammond
Andrea B. Mayfield*

DEDICATED TO:

Agnes and Robert Annis, who prepared and encouraged me to see the world through others' eyes. — *Sue*

Elizabeth, an author herself, Katie, who wants to name the elephant Susie, and Jeff for his unending support. — *Andrea*

THIN BOOK PUBLISHING CO

Business Manager: Rand Hammond
Designer: Jennifer Brower (www.dallasartists.com)
Illustrator: Dana Meek (www.almightyconcepts.com)

ISBN: 0-9665373-5-1

THIN BOOK PUBLISHING CO
86 SW CENTURY DR #446
BEND, OR 97702
888.316.9544
WWW.THINBOOK.COM

What You Are Going to Read

in the summer of 2003, we were working with a client organization on culture change. The future of the company depended on people behaving very differently. If they didn't change, they were going to go out of business. We were trying to help them understand how to change their organizational culture, a complex task at best. The concepts and measures we used just frustrated them further. *How can we possibly change an organization with 60,000 people scattered across the country in time to save our business?*, they asked.

We stopped and regrouped. We challenged ourselves as consultants. *How could we make this simpler?* After some experimentation and thought we both agreed that it was time to return to the basics. There are lots of books and theories about how organizations work, however, most people just need to know what small change they can make today. When we look at all the possibilities of what an organization can do to be more effective, it boils down to actually accessing more of what people already know. There are plenty of smart people working in organizations right now who have never offered their ideas about how to do things differently. People learn very quickly that it is better to be quiet than to speak up and look naïve, stupid or subversive. People truly fear for their jobs if they bring up the subject that no one is talking about, thus the saying: *There's an elephant in the room that everyone knows about but no one is acknowledging.*

*e*veryone talks around the elephant and thinks that *everyone else knows about the elephant*, but until the elephant's presence is made explicit, the level of dialogue — and therefore the quality of decision-making — is limited. The elephant stands for all the things no one talks about in an open forum. Make no mistake, people do talk about the elephant, but they do so at the proverbial water cooler, which is now electronic. The elephant is discussed in an unmanaged and potentially destructive, rather than constructive manner. People are fearful of naming the elephant because they are afraid they will lose their jobs or "face." However, not naming elephants can eat away at a person and at an organization. Unnamed elephants can pull the pillars away from your organization's foundational strengths, bringing down the entire structure. The real challenge is to decide which is more destructive: acknowledging the elephant to deal with it or ignoring it at your organization's peril.

The goal of this book is to show how to name elephants in a constructive way. We also want to convince you that it is imperative to do this because the consequences of not doing so can be disastrous. We believe that if you can build the skill, have a common language to do it, and the motivation to do it, you can begin to name elephants when the stakes are low. Once naming elephants becomes a comfortable practice for your organization, you will find people will do so when the stakes are higher.

think about it this way: You are sitting in a meeting and your stomach is flipping because you want to say something. You are afraid to say it because you might look like you don't know anything about what you are supposed to be an expert on. Yet you think the group is missing an important point. You're not sure because you only have one piece of the puzzle. You weigh the potential benefits of speaking up versus keeping quiet. If you keep quiet, no one will ever know what it is you are thinking.

Precisely our point ... no one will ever know what you are thinking. Multiply that by 60,000 people and you miss a lot of ideas, questions, data and knowledge. Yes, some of those ideas are unworkable. But we have all heard the stories of the great breakthroughs because someone had the persistence and courage to say aloud what was bothering them, and another person recognized the seed of a great idea or the avoidance of a disaster. As consultants, we believe our client organizations have vast quantities of untapped brilliance in the form of small statements or questions that name the elephant on everyone's mind. This book will show you how to name them and explain why it is important. We begin with a cautionary tale of how the un-named elephants at NASA created the environment which resulted in the tragedy of *Columbia*.

CHAPTER ONE

Lessons from Columbia

Americans learn only from catastrophes and not from experience.
— Theodore Roosevelt[1]
A crisis is a terrible thing to waste. — Paul Romer[2]

THE FOAM IS NOT A PROBLEM/THE FOAM IS THE CAUSE OF THE ACCIDENT

On February 1, 2003, the orbiter *Columbia* disintegrated over Texas and Louisiana. Seven astronauts lost their lives and two EPA employees later perished while searching for debris. To investigate the accident, NASA created the *Columbia* Accident Investigation Board (CAIB), which issued its report on August 26, 2003.

The report received widespread media coverage with headlines proclaiming NASA had a broken safety culture. As organizational behavior consultants, that headline caught our attention. The report is well-written, fascinating and potentially one of the best case studies currently available on organizational culture because of the rich detail. The following three key sentences jumped out at us:

- *"In our view, the NASA organizational culture had as much to do with this accident as the foam;*
- *NASA's initial briefings to the Board on its safety programs espoused a risk-averse philosophy that empowered any employee to stop an operation at the mere*

7

glimmer of a problem;

- *Unfortunately, NASA's view of its safety culture in those briefings did not reflect reality."*[3]

THE SAYING/DOING GAP

a foam strike on the wing during liftoff was the technical cause of the accident. The organizational culture contributed as *much* because NASA **said** it listened to all experts regardless of rank, while in reality it didn't, and NASA **wasn't aware** it wasn't listening. This represents the difference between **what organizations say they do and what they actually do.** The saying/doing gap is common to most organizations.[4] It takes concentrated effort for organizations to be aware of this difference, and it is often a critical factor between organizational success and failure.

MULTIPLE REALITIES

Organizations are also not always aware that there are different interpretations of what is said or done because of the notion of **multiple concurrent realities**. That means people can see the same thing at the same time in completely different ways. We've all been to a meeting where participants later describe it in such different ways that we ask, were we even at the same meeting? The reason is that every individual sees and hears through his or her own personal filters. In an effort to keep the world manageable, people often see what they want to see and ignore information that does not fit their preconceptions. People seek stability and security, and seeing things in a way that conforms to their beliefs gives them both.

CATEGORIES

the amount of data in the world can be overwhelming, so we create categories to group data to make it easier to understand. Crickets may not fit in your category called *food* unless you're lost in the wild and hungry. Then crickets might look tasty. We often toss things into those pre-defined categories — sometimes without any conscious thought. When information shows up that threatens our comfortable view of the world, we become anxious and defensive. If we are too anxious, we deny or ignore the existence of the new information. In their excellent book *Managing the Unexpected*, Karl Weick and Kathleen Sutcliffe explain multiple realities this way:

"The trouble starts when I fail to notice that I see only whatever confirms my categories and expectations but nothing else. The trouble deepens even further if I kid myself that seeing is believing. That's wrong. It's the other way around. You see what you expect to see. You see what you have the labels to see. You see what you have the skills to manage. Everything else is a blur. And in that 'everything else' lies the developing unexpected event that can bite you and undermine your best intentions."[5]

9

YOU SEE WHAT YOU EXPECT TO SEE

We don't want to explore the potentially ugly news that our product is no longer competitive, so we seek out and hear only the positives. We stop reassessing and reevaluating and depend on our past definitions of reality until overwhelming evidence forces us to revise and update our view of the world. Yet the disciplined process of review and reevaluation is the basis for potential competitive advantage. If you can gather up all the different points of view of your diverse employees (multiple concurrent realities), you create more probability that you (collectively) will see new opportunities for your organization. But in the overwhelming busyness of the 24/7 week, we default to the shortcut of "seeing" things the same way. We stop debating "reality."

Not taking the time to look at reality with fresh eyes can also result in what is called the "normalization of deviance."[6] We found this intriguing phrase in Diane Vaughn's book on the *Challenger* accident. It is used to explain how something that is a slight deviation from the expected result begins to be viewed as normal or acceptable if it happens often enough. When explaining the concept to a client with a small retail business, the client realized that she had normalized shoplifting. Shoplifting isn't normal behavior. However, if it happens enough and you feel powerless to stop it, you begin to categorize it as an accepted expense of a retail business. Another client began to normalize their less-than-expected sales results. They slowly continued to adjust their sales forecasts down until they almost went out of business. It took a new chairman to force the organization to see the new reality that they were in trouble.

nASA had a process that in essence normalized deviance by creating categories to decide how to handle unexpected results. When you consider the enormous amount of data NASA must review, you can understand why it needed categories. Any deviation from the expected was evaluated and dropped into a category. Depending on the category, certain procedures were followed. The most important category was called *affecting safety of flight*. Anything that fell into this category had to be dealt with, meaning action had to be taken. Foam strikes were not meant to occur. However, they did occur repeatedly over the course of 22 years without any serious safety consequences. The first foam strike was evaluated and placed into a category called *turnaround*, meaning the event affected the time it took to get the shuttle ready to fly again. The turnaround category isn't as ominous as the safety-of-flight category, so action can be deferred.

11

FACTS

foam strikes continued to occur in later flights, but because they had been previously categorized as turnaround, it became much more difficult to get people to review whether this was still a proper label. NASA, one of our chief scientific institutions, had not tested its hypothesis that foam strikes were not dangerous. **The belief that foam strikes were not a safety-of-flight issue became a fact because on prior flights foam strikes did not cause serious consequences.** Anecdotal stories become operating facts when told often enough and when an organization does not take the time to question underlying assumptions. NASA did not have a regular reassessment of categories in place. When the engineers tried to reexamine the reality that foam strikes might affect flight safety, they were told a reexamination wasn't necessary.

12

Facts also develop when someone in a position of power unintentionally creates a "fact." For example, the senior leader at NASA who made the comment in an email that the impact of the foam strikes "should not be a problem"[7] probably did so without realizing that others heard it as a fact. People began to make decisions based on what was never intended to be anything other than a casual observation in an email. We call this the **whisper becomes a scream** effect. People who are perceived as having power should understand how their voices become amplified through their positions and be purposeful about what they say.

I t takes dedicated initiative and perseverance to overcome the momentum of prior categorization. If people are punished for taking this initiative, they begin to keep their concerns to themselves. Thus the unnamed elephant lurks in the corner. The best way to make this clear is to teach people to do a gut check. If your gut tells you something is wrong or amiss or just not quite what you expected, pay attention. An elephant may be lurking, and chances are you are not the only one who senses it.

LOOKING BACK WITH 20/20 HINDSIGHT

Prior to the *Columbia* and *Challenger* accidents, NASA had a proud history of accomplishments.[8] It certainly had many more successes than failures in its 40-year history. Over that period, NASA also experienced what most organizations do in their lifecycle: a change in mission. It went from the thrill of putting a man on the moon in 1969 to creating and maintaining reusable orbiters on a predetermined launch schedule with a limited budget. NASA also gained an administrator who dealt with the organization's budget and strategic challenges by exhorting people to do things "faster, better, cheaper."

t he change in mission and the "faster, better, cheaper" mantra created a shift in NASA's culture. For example, by trying to run meetings in what was intended to be an efficient and timely manner, managers shut down exploratory dialogue of highly skilled engineers. This focus on operational efficiency and meeting predetermined launch schedules was more apropos for an airline with regularly scheduled flights than for an agency sending astronauts into space. It is important to note that these slight shifts in behavior did not occur through intentional organizational design. Individuals began to change their old ways, thinking they could meet the faster, better, cheaper objectives. As a result, NASA lost one of its original core competencies, which astronaut Sally Ride describes as being "inquisitive to a fault."[9] Ride, also a member of the CAIB, puts it this way:

"Faster, better, cheaper, when applied to the human space program, was not a productive concept. It was a false economy. It's very difficult to have all three simultaneously. Pick your favorite two. With human space flight, you'd better add the word 'safety' in there too because if upper management is going 'faster, better, cheaper,' that percolates down and it puts the emphasis on meeting schedules and improving the way that you do things and on cost. And over the years, it provides the impression that budget and schedule are the most important things." [10]

We can't fault NASA managers' attempt to be efficient without taking into consideration just how complex and

14

ambiguous their environment is. In some ways NASA had come to resemble a typical Fortune 500 company. It no longer had unlimited resources or the overwhelming support of the public and Congress, it didn't have a clear strategic mission, and it had decentralized enough to lose the big picture when it came to problem-solving. Therefore individuals made trade-offs between production pressure and safety concerns without realizing they were doing it. Not only were the saying/doing gaps large, there were also huge differences in how different teams saw reality, and they never took the time to compare their views. The efficiency goal overwhelmed the stated value of being curious to a fault.

t he CAIB declared NASA's safety culture broken in 2003 because the cause of the *Columbia* accident was similar to the cause of the *Challenger* accident 17 years earlier. A crisis is an opportunity for an organization to learn, and unfortunately NASA had not applied the lessons from *Challenger*. A key finding from the *Challenger* accident investigation was that there was intense political pressure to **not** delay the launch due to the high profile of the flight.[11] Meeting the launch schedule became more important than being inquisitive about why the engineers with the most expertise on the O-rings had reservations about launching *Challenger* in lower-than-normal temperatures. The engineers had concerns about the safety of the flight. They didn't believe they had enough evidence to understand the potential impact of the low temperatures on the O-rings. The engineers had identified the "mere glimmer of a problem." However, in direct contrast to NASA's stated value that all employees were empowered to stop the operation, the engineers were cut out of the decision-making process by higher-level managers intent on meeting the schedule.

the Debris Assessment Team, in charge of reviewing the potential damage of foam or any debris strikes on *Columbia*, was inquisitive to a fault. On the morning of January 17, 2003, this team reviewed the videos of the launch and saw something that concerned them. They **saw something new because they were open to new information or new configurations of information.** They were looking for **differences between expected results and actual results** and interpreting the potential consequences of each of these differences. The Debris Assessment Team did not assume that foam strikes were normal and harmless.

16

They also believed that the foam striking *Columbia's* wing on liftoff appeared bigger and had hit at a higher rate of velocity than any previous foam strike. Despite the fact that foam strikes had not yet caused an accident,[12] any debris strike can potentially create a hole in the wing which could cause a burn-through on reentry. The Debris Assessment Team took their concerns about these foam strikes seriously and went into action to obtain images of the wing from either the Department of Defense satellites or high-resolution cameras from the ground. They took the initiative to request the images **but went outside of the chain of command.** Because of the rigid hierarchy at NASA, which NASA denied it had, going outside the chain of command proved to be a disastrous decision. When the manager in charge heard about the back-channel request (which should have been cleared through her), she responded with efficient bureaucracy. She checked it out with her peers but not with the team that had made the request. Based on what her peers told her, she canceled the request for imagery **without any discussion with the team that initiated the request.**

ccording to William Langewiesche in a riveting article in *The Atlantic Monthly,*[13] the "NASA liaison officer then emailed an apology to the Air Force personnel, assuring them that the shuttle was in 'excellent shape' and explaining that a foam strike was 'something that has happened before and is not considered to be a major problem.'" His next comment is telling: "The one problem that this has identified is the need for some additional coordination within NASA to assure that when a request is made it is done through the official channels." **In other words, the problem they "saw" wasn't the potential danger**

17

of the foam strike. They defined the problem as NASA employees' going around the hierarchy to get information about something that they considered in the category of affecting the safety of the flight. Instead of debating the potential consequences of the foam strike, the managers were concerned their power was being usurped.

I n most organizations, the consequence of a rigid hierarchy isn't the loss of human life. However, overly rigid hierarchies generally do not welcome new information that threatens the status quo. As a result, they discourage employees from speaking up, and from looking for new configurations of facts. **This cultural rigidity always has a steep price for the organization. We call this cost the Price of Passivity.**

DIDN'T ANYONE SPEAK UP?

Several engineers persisted in raising their concerns about the foam, only to be finally told by the higher-ups that the foam was not a problem. The engineers backed off. When asked why, they explained they feared for their jobs. Admiral Gehman, the director of the CAIB, explains NASA's culture in Langewiesche's article:

"They claim that the culture in Houston is a 'badgeless society' meaning it doesn't matter what you have on your badge — you're concerned about shuttle safety together. **Well, that's all nice, but the truth is that it does matter what badge you're wearing ... .But then**

when you look at how it really works, it's an incestuous, hierarchi-
cal system, with invisible rankings and a very strict informal chain of
command. They all know that. So even though they've got all the trap-
pings of communication, you don't actually find communication ... . But if
a person brings an issue up, what caste he's in makes all the difference.
Now again, NASA will deny this, but if you talk to people, if you re-
ally listen to people, all the time you hear 'Well, I was afraid to speak
up.' Boy it comes across loud and clear. You listen to the meetings:
'Anybody got anything to say?' There are thirty people in the room,
and slam! There's nothing. We have plenty of witness statements saying
'If I had spoken up, it would have been at the cost of my job.'"14

THE ORGANIZATION AS A SYSTEM

mistakes are made, accidents occur,
communications are stilted but not typically
through malicious intent. There isn't
one person to blame for either accident; the underlying
contributing cause was how people reacted to each other
within the organizational system. The system failed to
explore why mistakes happened and what could be learned.
Organizational theorist Barry Oshry explains an organizational
system through the terms Tops, Middles and Bottoms. He
describes how "in systems we exist only in relationship to
one another."15 The Tops are supposed to set the vision,
the Middles organize, and the Bottoms do, and typically,
individuals unconsciously follow those roles. When we

19

reviewed the CAIB, it appeared that the vision set by the Tops at NASA was to meet the launch schedule "faster, better, cheaper." The Middles kept things on track in what they defined as an efficient manner. The Bottoms handled the technical details. The Middles tried to keep meetings moving, so when they asked if anyone had any comments, they did so because it seemed to be a good way to be thorough. However, they really didn't expect to hear any comments or concerns that would disturb the efficiency of the schedule. The Bottoms knew that and kept quiet.

Instead, the Bottoms communicated their concerns in subtle ways — through email, through abbreviated PowerPoint slides, and through back-channel requests. They acted as if they were not supposed to bring up any concerns unless they had proof. This is in direct contrast to being inquisitive to a fault and the stated belief that "any employee was empowered to stop an operation at the mere glimmer of a problem."[16] The Tops had over time — and perhaps inadvertently — created an unspoken requirement that those lower in the organization **prove** their concerns in advance. In other words, people were expected not to bring up bad news unless they were absolutely sure it was bad news.

THE UNDISCUSSABLES

What happened at NASA was the gradual shift from the stated value that anyone sensing a "mere glimmer of a problem" could stop an operation to an actual practice that only Tops could make that decision. The shift also created what organizational theorist Chris Argyris calls an **undiscussable** and what we call an *unnamed elephant*. Subjects that are undiscussable in organizations become so in order to "avoid surprise, embarrassment or threat."[17] An undiscussable is a taboo subject, something people don't talk about in an open forum. One key impact of the Web is that many organizations now have websites where people do discuss the undiscussables, although generally anonymously. The problem with that is that the undiscussables still aren't dealt with in an open forum.

Several subjects became undiscussables at NASA: the role of hierarchy over expertise, for example. Instead of the so-called badgeless system, there was extreme sensitivity to where each person stood in the hierarchy. The rules about when each person was allowed to speak given their rank in the hierarchy were also not discussed in an open forum. We surmise the following were undiscussables at NASA:

21

- The negative impact of the hierarchical system on decision-making;
- The stated values (safety) were not the actual values in practice (faster, better, cheaper);
- There were trappings of communication, but no real communication;
- Who you are in the caste system makes a difference (Tops, Middles, and Bottoms);
- A fear of criticism by peers for speaking up without proof; and
- A fear of job loss after delivering bad news.

Unfortunately, we believe this list reflects undiscussables common to many organizations. The result of allowing a culture of undiscussables is that new information gets blocked. There is often little or no tolerance for facts that potentially disturb the status quo. This limits the understanding of trends that may impact the organization's future success. For example, NASA made foam an undiscussable, Detroit automakers made Japanese cars an undiscussable, Xerox made Japanese copiers an undiscussable, IBM made Apple an undiscussable, American Airlines made Southwest Airlines an undiscussable, Kodak made digital photography an undiscussable, and more recently the entire music industry made MP3 file-sharing an undiscussable.

t he reason undiscussables or unnamed elephants are so dangerous to an organization is that they shut down the possibility of taking advantage of new trends before the competition does. Andy Grove, former chairman of Intel, addressed the subject in his book aptly entitled *Only the Paranoid Survive: How to Exploit the Crisis Points That Challenge Every Company and Career.* "[Grove] emphasized the importance of recognizing change early, especially with help from people he describes as Cassandras, named after the priestess who foretold the fall of Troy."[18]

LISTENING TO CASSANDRAS

Every industry and organization faces constant technological or competitive breakthroughs that potentially threaten their business. The key to keeping a competitive edge is to notice the small signals or trends before they become big problems. Or, to flip to the constructive view thoroughly discussed by Jim Collins in *Good To Great*, great companies notice the small trends and find a way to exploit them to their advantage.[19]

23

For example, Starbucks recently took action to add a service on its website that allows customers to download Starbucks' popular playlists. It spotted and responded to the trend because employees reported that customers were asking for a list of what was playing in the store. This action is both a service to its customers and an opportunity for revenue (selling more CDs). Starbucks is an example of a company that benefits by seeking out and respectfully listening to the views and ideas of all the people in its organization, regardless of rank. The company expects all of its employees to "create a community" by welcoming people into each store, learning frequent customers' names, and anticipating their favorite drinks. Starbucks realizes that one employee can either positively or negatively affect a customer's experience in a very subtle way.

It is those closest to the customers (or the Bottoms in most organizations) who have the most opportunity to notice trends, a practice called environmental scanning. An effective organization doesn't have to wait for the marketing department to identify a new product. It actively seeks out the opinions and ideas of all its employees. Contrast that with a more rigid hierarchy that sends a message that the Bottoms have little of value to offer. The result of the rigid hierarchy is that the scope of scanning becomes narrower or nonexistent or dependent on outside research. We have yet to find an organization that complains it has too many new ideas for products or services. Unfortunately, we rarely see an organization with a disciplined practice of seeking out the ideas of those closest to the customer. In fact, the Bottoms are usually belittled as not being smart or savvy enough to spot a trend. The Bottoms get the message and keep quiet.

Southwest Airlines is another organization that has been successful at listening to its employees. It also dedicates substantial organizational resources to maintaining its culture and values. The entire business model depends on employees, at all levels, not only getting along, but actively helping and communicating with each other. The company begins by selecting people with a certain attitude, and Southwest has successfully defended its right to fire people who aren't "nice." The company also has a six-month probationary period that it takes very seriously. If someone doesn't fit, Southwest lets them go. One pilot applicant was rude to a reservation agent and found his interview canceled for that reason. At Southwest, turnaround time is so tight that pilots often help clean the planes — they cannot hold themselves above anyone else in the organization. Instead of providing employees with a thick policy manual, the company expects people to "follow the golden rule" because it answers every question they may have.

25

KEY LEVERAGE POINTS

It may seem overly simple, but we propose that paying attention to what people talk about and what they don't talk about is often an overlooked key to organizational success. Add to that, creating a conscious awareness of who is allowed to speak and who is expected to stay silent and you have two powerful leverage points to create a more effective organization. Open, inclusive dialogue should be a core competency. Including the views of all organizational levels in the discipline expands your knowledge base exponentially. To take advantage of these leverage points, your organizational culture must encourage people to do the following:

- Speak up and share any concern or idea;
- Respectfully disagree or agree to disagree;
- Share and debate multiple realities;
- Question those in power;
- Explore many alternatives before shutting down discussion or making decisions; and
- Take turns playing devil's advocate or the contrarian.

none of these processes were present in NASA's culture in February, 2003. Somehow NASA had gone from the famous "Houston, we have a problem" safety culture that saved *Apollo 13* to a broken safety culture. We know that people don't come to work intending to shut down communication through a caste system, and we know that to a person, everyone at NASA is committed to flight safety. How is it that no one spoke up until disaster struck? And who is not speaking up in your organization?

In the next chapter we show you how to encourage people to speak up.

!

USE THESE QUESTIONS TO CREATE CONVERSATION IN YOUR WORK GROUP

- What are our undiscussables?
- What is it we didn't talk about today that we should have?
- What information do we have that contradicts our current beliefs?
- How many people spoke up to present information that challenged the status quo at our last meeting?
- How does our hierarchy work for us? How does it get in the way?
- What categories do we use or overuse?
- Who is our "Cassandra"?
- How do I view myself: as a Top, Middle or Bottom?

!

EXAMPLES OF THE SAYING/DOING GAP AT NASA[20]

- *What they said they believed*
  All voices are equal.
- *How they behaved*
  The higher you are in rank, the more important your voice.

- *What they said they believed*
  If you have a safety concern, you should share it.
- *How they behaved*
  Don't share your safety concern unless you can prove it's a safety concern.

- *What they said they believed*
  Safety of flight is our most important concern.
- *How they behaved*
  Meeting our external flight schedule is our most important concern.

29

UNNAMED ELEPHANTS ON THE LOOSE

YOUR COMPANY

CHAPTER TWO

Naming the Elephant

Organizations work very hard at silencing people.
— *Karlene Kerfoot*[21]

t he first step in learning what people are talking about and not talking about is to understand the difference between implicit and explicit communication. We call it *naming the elephant* because of the expression, *there's an elephant in the room and no one is talking about it.*[24] The elephant is implicit and an undiscussable. Everyone talks around the elephant and thinks that *everyone else knows about the elephant.* But until the elephant's presence is made explicit, the level of dialogue — and therefore the quality of decision-making — is limited. Naming the elephant is a metaphor for making implicit issues explicit. **In our work with organizations, we have learned that naming the elephant and discussing how each individual sees the elephant are often overlooked keys to good decision-making and innovation.**

31

Over twenty-five years ago, Jerry Harvey wrote a classic article about this called "The Abilene Paradox: The Management of Agreement."[25] A family is sitting around on a hot Sunday when the father proposes a trip to Abilene for lunch because he thinks they are bored. They all think the others want to go and they all "say" they want to go although they would just as soon sit on the porch and play checkers. Once they return from the hot, dusty trip, they finally have an explicit discussion in which they each admit that they had not wanted to go in the first place. They named the elephant after they wasted the afternoon. It's not as if the consequences were so terrible, but Dr. Harvey points out that organizations make the trip to Abilene over and over because they don't communicate on an explicit level.

HOW DO YOU NAME ELEPHANTS?

naming elephants is a three-part process. First, identify what is undiscussable, or name the elephant. Second, surface the underlying assumptions people have about the elephant or the situation. This creates the opportunity to view all the ways people see the reality of the situation (multiple realities). Third, learn how to have constructive dialogue involving Tops, Middles and Bottoms. We want to emphasize that this is not a linear process and can happen in any order. Dialogue is often the time the elephant is named or the assumptions are surfaced. The key is to include constructive dialogue somewhere in the process because dialogue techniques can dissipate the fear created by power and status differentials. Power and status differentials always have a huge impact on people's willingness to openly explore different points of view. We have repeatedly observed the most assertive Middles become passive when they enter into a conversation with Tops. When we ask them later why they didn't speak up, they almost always respond that they were

afraid of something — from looking stupid or uninformed
to looking like they were trying to get attention, or worse,
to being labeled a troublemaker. Most organizations would
benefit from developing or increasing their competency in
dialogue or having what authors, Stone, Patton and Heen call
Difficult Conversations and Scott calls *Fierce Conversations.*[26]

a long with naming elephants and constructive dialogue
is the step of surfacing the assumptions everyone
brings to their view of the world. Creating a discipline
of actively surfacing and examining assumptions with a diverse
group of people is a key leverage point for success in any
knowledge organization. This practice creates the opportunity
to debate the multiple realities, allowing the group to find the
nuances that lead to competitive breakthroughs.

WHAT ARE ASSUMPTIONS?

Assumptions are beliefs about how the world works. We create
them throughout our lives, through the filter of our unique
set of experiences and education. Assumptions are sometimes
called frame of reference, mind-set, worldview, point of view,
mental model, operating assumption, belief, lens, conventional
wisdom, context, our story, values or "the way we do things
around here." Assumptions are:

33

- Statements or rules that explain what a person or group generally believes;
- Developed over time and eventually become invisible or implicit; and
- Created out of a human need for stability.

WHY ARE ASSUMPTIONS IMPORTANT?

Assumptions create a template through which we view the world. Any group that forms to achieve a united purpose agrees to a common set of assumptions, usually in the beginning or *norming* stage of the group. This shared set of assumptions causes the group to think and act in certain ways and represents the common sense of the group. **The longer the assumptions are in effect, and the more success the group has, the harder it is for the group to see any new information that contradicts its beliefs.** The beauty of assumptions is they become shorthand for the group. When faced with similar situations, a group just acts (or reacts) and doesn't need to reevaluate why each time.

34

Over time the group's assumptions operate at an unconscious level, allowing the group to work efficiently without constantly stopping to determine what they believe and therefore how they should act. The downside is that the group may **fail to notice new data that contradicts its beliefs and may miss an opportunity to**

improve effectiveness. This is why it is important to bring to the surface and evaluate group assumptions every so often to see if they are still valid.

I n *The Reckoning*, David Halberstam describes how the once-mighty Detroit auto industry missed the emergence of the trend of fuel-efficient cars during the energy crisis of the Seventies.[27] Halberstam reports that automakers only looked in their own parking lots to assess the popularity of their cars. Based on what they saw, they assumed that the cars they made were attractive to their customers. The automakers also assumed that Americans would never give up their love affair with the big gas guzzlers. They should have questioned the assumption that what was in their parking lots or what they saw driving around Detroit reflected the reality of the entire country. Had they been open to looking outside Detroit, they might have noticed that West Coast customers' were buying fuel efficient cars as they were unloaded from Japan.

35

But the auto industry of the Seventies believed that its assumptions were valid and didn't need to be discussed or debated. In author Andy Grove's terms, the automakers stopped being paranoid. The result was a crushing loss of market share. In *The End of Detroit*, author Micheline Maynard explores how 40 years ago, "nine in ten automobile sales in the United States were built in Detroit."[28] By 2003, the number was down to only six in ten vehicles. It is interesting to note that in the last few years, Americans have returned to their first love of gas guzzlers by embracing SUVs. Americans really did not want to give up gas guzzlers — they started buying them again when they felt they could afford the gas. This time, Detroit was on top of the trend by producing the very profitable trucks and SUVs. This example shows how important it is to constantly reevaluate and reassess the validity of the assumptions on which you base your business decisions.

HOW DO YOU SURFACE ASSUMPTIONS?

the only way to check out the current value of an assumption is to surface it or make it visible to all the team members and then open it up for discussion. One way we do this is to use a survival simulation to show people how to surface assumptions and practice on an example that isn't about their own business or industry. In most survival simulations, you are given a list of items and have to decide first as an individual and then as a group which items will help you survive. The best chance the group has to survive is to pool knowledge and compare assumptions, thus creating a larger pool of knowledge to make a more informed decision. We ask that individuals first read the situation and then write out their assumptions by completing this statement: **I assume that _____ because_____.** For example, "I assume that I need the car to escape the fire because I can drive out of here." Survival simulations are fun, low-risk ways to show that every person has a different set of assumptions that may or may not be valid. After they write out their assumptions and rank the items in order of importance, participants are supposed to share both their assumptions and their ranking with the group. We instruct the group to come to a consensus on its ranking.

decision-making processes in many organizations do not include the step of surfacing and comparing assumptions. As a result, we have found that on average at least half the groups ignore the directions and instead begin to practice typical hierarchical bureaucratic behavior. For example, they do the following:

- They immediately begin to limit full participation;
- Usually a hierarchy of Tops, Middles and Bottoms is quickly and implicitly established. It may reflect their actual rank, or it may reflect claimed expertise. The one or two Tops assert their status by intimidating others. They stand up and grab the marker and begin to take control of the group. They assert their power with complete confidence that they know what is right;
- They imply or state that other participants are wrong. ("You're crazy, I'm going to survive, and you're already dead.");

37

- They avoid a full discussion of various alternatives and immediately proceed to a vote; and
- They finish early and wonder what is taking the other groups so long to get to the obvious answer.

the groups that follow our directions to compare their assumptions invariably surface new information. It's amazing how creative solutions are when people actually take time to listen respectfully to each other's beliefs. They describe the process as "understanding where the other person is coming from." The score of the groups who take the time to do this is almost always better than the average individual decision score. That means they did better as a group than they would have as individuals, which confirms that some learning took place at the group level. **This is how organizations make breakthroughs: They surface and recombine information in new ways to create new products or services or see new possibilities by looking at something differently.**

38

Oftentimes, it is a humbling but excellent learning experience for the groups that replicate the bureaucracy. Their decision-making process is fractured as they align with those who agree with them and distance themselves from those who don't. After they hear what the other teams did, they often have an "ah-hah" moment. Practicing the skill of surfacing assumptions through a simulation is a low-risk way to examine the process people use under stress. Once people see why taking the time to surface assumptions is valuable, they begin to incorporate the process when they make more important decisions.

CONSTRUCTIVE DIALOGUE

the third step is to learn how to have constructive dialogue, which creates an open and respectful forum for discussing different views, realities and formerly taboo subjects. It is the place people learn to agree to disagree without shutting down future conversations. Most organizations are used to practicing advocacy instead of inquiry in their conversations. Advocacy is a win-lose form of communication that doesn't respect multiple realities. In an advocacy frame, each person is trying to convince the other that he or she is right, and that there is only one right answer. Dialogue is a form of inquiry that assumes people see the world differently. In a dialogue frame, each person assumes he or she can learn something new from others and become better informed as a result.

39

There are many different techniques for achieving constructive dialogue,[29] but here is a basic description of a dialogue process. First, get the right people in the room. The Debris Assessment Team at NASA should have been invited to have an open dialogue with the Middles who were making the decisions. By sitting face-to-face and following this type of process, the

Middles would have had a greater chance of hearing the new evidence and seeing the concerns of the Debris Assessment Team.

the dialogue begins by naming the issue or defining what they are there to discuss. The group should list all the assumptions on a flip chart or white board (so everyone can see them), working around the room to include each person's contribution. To alleviate power and status issues, the group should take the approach that each assumption is valid and list the "what if" consequences. For example, *if the foam strike did damage the wing and there is a potential for a burn-through on reentry, then the orbiter may be destroyed.* This should be done with each assumption in a brainstorming ("there are no bad ideas") manner. It also helps if you don't allow the most senior person in the room to do the recording and you rotate this responsibility.

40

Then the group should reverse the discussion and approach each assumption as if it were not valid and list those "what if" consequences. One person in the group should be assigned the devil's advocate or contrarian role to make sure everything is questioned. That role should be rotated among group members so people experience what it feels like to question the status quo. Another member of the group should be assigned the role of facilitator, making sure each person speaks. If someone doesn't have anything to add, he or she should say "pass." It is important to formalize the norm that every person is expected to speak. By going around the table taking turns, you will limit the most vocal person (and there is one in every group) who wants to dominate.

essentially, constructive dialogue is about people talking to each other in a respectful manner that allows information to be shared and acted on. People take turns talking and no one is allowed to interrupt. Dialogue assumes that all participants have something valuable to offer. It also depends on a certain level of trust. If information is hoarded because knowledge is power, people won't share. If there is a highly oppositional organizational culture — where personal attacks are allowed or when the loudest person wins — people will duck and become quiet. The competency of being open to different points of view and **creating an environment that respects and expects everyone's unique point of view can be developed through constructive dialogue.** We believe that you never know where the million-dollar idea is hiding in someone's unspoken idea, so it is imperative to create a climate of trust and dialogue.

41

REACH RESOLUTION

Constructive dialogue shouldn't be an excuse to have endless discussion and not come to a conclusion. Ultimately, decisions need to be made along with agreement on next steps and how and when there will be follow-up. Every meeting should try to end with a To-Do List. Our clients tell us that coming to some kind of conclusion is the most challenging part of their attempt to actually execute. However, you have a better chance of buy-in to decisions if everyone who is close to the situation has participated in the decision-making process. You will also have a better decision if you have heard everyone's point of view. Realizing that consensus may not be reached, many organizations have a two-step process: If they don't reach a consensus, they designate a decision-maker.

EXECUTE

In an organization, it is never enough to just talk about it; someone has to execute the plan. But to get beyond talk to decision-making, apprehensions must be addressed. Research shows that people have the following concerns about decisions: [30]

- Are they made fairly?
- Whose interests were served?
- Are costs and benefits equitably distributed?
- Why this decision and not another?
- Who assumed the role of decision-maker, and why?

if they have answers to these questions, people will execute. Execution is imperative — a book topic in itself. **No organization can survive without actually doing what it says it is going to do and holding people accountable.**

SUCCESSFUL ORGANIZATIONS

What kind of organizations show competency in naming elephants, surfacing assumptions and constructive dialogue? Weick and Sutcliff share the success factors of what are called High Reliability Organizations (HROs) in their book, *Managing the Unexpected*.[31] Unlike organizations that avoid surfacing or discussing surprises, High Reliability Organizations are good at looking for and managing the unexpected. These organizations are deeply attuned to — some might say obsessed with — studying any blip on the screen, any deviance from the expected. For the most part, they work in complex, often fast-paced and highly technical environments and are called High Reliability Organizations because they have fewer than their fair share of problems. This is a good thing for the rest of us because HROs include nuclear aircraft carriers, nuclear generating plants, air traffic control systems and hospital emergency rooms.

Perhaps these organizations are reliable because the consequences are so high. In any of these environments little mistakes can quickly escalate into potentially deadly results. Success in these organizations means they not only avoid accidents but are actively, as Weick and Sutcliffe describe it, "preoccupied with their failures." Potential accidents are studied, reviewed and used as learning vehicles rather than becoming undiscussables. **People in High Reliability Organizations are rewarded for pointing out any deviation from the expected. This is the exact opposite of most hierarchical organizations, that "shoot" the messenger who brings potentially bad news.**

Weick and Sutcliffe also note that managers in HROs know the difference between consensus created because everyone has the same assumptions or is unwilling to speak up for fear of their jobs and consensus created because all the assumptions have been surfaced and discussed. **They understand that ignorance and knowledge grow at the same rate because the more you know, the more you know you don't know.** That is why if you include every person's view of reality, you have a greater potential to capture all the possibilities. This is why we stress paying attention to who is included in your discussions. Great companies understand that diversity of thought represents multiple concurrent realities and they use it to their advantage. Instead of asking "Does anyone have anything to say?" they go around the room and expect everyone to say something — and the more contrarian, the better. This requires a leadership style that believes that all organizational members have something valuable to offer, especially the Bottoms, who are closest to the doing and therefore the surprises.

Unlike NASA's supposedly badgeless culture with its caste system, High Reliability Organizations are hierarchies that when faced with a crisis, flex to take advantage of all relevant expertise, regardless of rank. In fact, in a crisis situation, decision-making in HROs "migrates" to the experts needed for that issue. If an alarm is raised about foam, the decision-making power migrates to the engineers who know the most about foam. If an alarm is raised about O-rings, the decision-making power migrates to the engineers who know the most about O-rings. During a crisis, **the hierarchy doesn't step in to protect their rank and status; instead they step aside to support the most relevant expertise to make sense of the surprise or the potential of a bad outcome.**

45

High Reliability Organizations work from a fear mentality, but it is the fear of the potential consequences of "little mistakes that escalate."[32] HROs successfully remove the personal fear of people losing their jobs if they speak up, and convert it to the fear of what may happen to others (possibly many others) if they don't speak up. HROs are organizations where people actively look for and imagine what could go wrong and trust their instincts without having to prove something first. **The result is that no one person has to figure it all out on their own; they know they can rely on others.** Being able to rely on others — pooling knowledge — is the key advantage for anyone to join an organization.

HOW INQUISITIVE CAN AN ORGANIZATION AFFORD TO BE?

t he question is how many resources can you dedicate to naming elephants, surfacing assumptions and having constructive dialogue? Organizations depend on their assumptions in order to have a "workable level of certainty."[33] This means that people need to be able to make daily decisions without stopping and reexamining their entire set of assumptions. **You may argue that your organization can't take the time to review all assumptions; however, we believe organizations need to spend more time surfacing and examining assumptions in order to open themselves to a greater number of possibilities.** Weick puts it this way: "Organizations that both believe and doubt their past experience retain more flexibility and adaptive capacity."[34] Simultaneous belief and doubt lead to constructive dialogue or a "good fight," which Jim Collins reports is a core competency of companies that have gone from good to great.[35]

Collins describes the good fight as involving as many people as possible in order to make the best decision possible — not just come to consensus, which may indicate a watered-down decision — and have the greatest amount of buy-in to the decision so that it is actually executed. Too many organizations complain that decisions they thought were agreed upon were later sabotaged by those who had not understood the decision in the first place because the good fight didn't happen. When people don't feel heard or don't understand why a decision was made, they have less investment in executing.

Also, a huge amount of organizational time is wasted in what a colleague calls *the meeting before the meeting, the meeting, and the meeting after the meeting to strategize how to not do or undo what was decided in the meeting.*[36] For those who say they don't have time to get everyone into the room to have a good fight, we suggest calculating what it actually costs to have all these before and after meetings. Figure out the average hourly rate of each person in the room and multiply it by the time spent in meetings to determine your "burn rate." In one client group, we calculated a burn rate of $5,000 an hour for a particular group. This retail client calculated how many pairs of socks

47

they had to sell to pay for that one-hour meeting. That made the cost of unnecessary meetings real.

*a*t NASA, the cause of both the *Columbia* and *Challenger* accidents was that the good fight never occurred. The discussions were shut down prematurely by proclamations by the Tops, and accepted by the Middles and Bottoms because of the culture that had been created and maintained at NASA. The CAIB report also describes why the good fight is so important:

"It is obvious but worth acknowledging, that people who are marginal and powerless in organizations may have useful information or opinions that they don't express. Even when these people are encouraged to speak, they find it intimidating to contradict a leader's strategy or a group consensus. Extra effort must be made to contribute all relevant information to discussions of risk. These strategies are important for all safety aspects, but especially necessary for ill-structured problems like O-rings and foam debris. Because ill-structured problems are less visible and therefore invite the normalization of deviance, they may be the most risky of all."[37]

SWIMMING UPSTREAM

What gets in the way of inclusive, respectful dialogue? We've seen groups created in organizations that are successful at having good fights, surfacing assumptions and making positive, constructive recommendations. They are sometimes

called advisory boards, quality circles, employee action teams
or tiger teams. They present their findings to management
and everyone agrees that they are good ideas. Then nothing
happens. Why? The Tops are trapped in the system and can't
figure out how to change the system enough to implement
new ideas. The system fights any new idea because it disturbs
the status quo. It takes great perseverance to change an
organization. Without strong commitment, the system
reverts to its old ways at the first sign of a crisis. With the
current velocity of the environment, crises happen every
day. Implementing change in this kind of environment takes
constant vigilance, mindfulness and commitment to integrate
new ideas. It takes a daily discipline of naming elephants. We
tell our clients that they can't wait until the entire organization
changes. Change in any organization happens one person at a
time.

I n the next chapter we will address the unnamed elephants
that we believe get in the way of creating more great
companies.

!

CONVERSATION STARTERS

- When did we last surface our assumptions for discussion?
- What do we as an organization/department/ team get defensive about?
- Do we currently expect all members of the organization to speak up? Do we reward them when they do? Or do we shut them down?
- How do we close the loop on talk and make sure deadlines are set and followed up on?

!

CONVERSATION STARTERS (CONTINUED)

- How often do we "go to Abilene" and why?
- How do we exhibit our inquisitiveness? Are we curious to a fault?
- What does our organization both believe and doubt at the same time?
- What is our meeting burn rate?
- When is the last time we successfully integrated a new idea, and how did we do it?

UNNAMED ELEPHANTS ON THE LOOSE

YOUR COMPANY

CHAPTER THREE

Naming the Elephants of Hubris, Arrogance and Screamers

The beauty and the frightening quality of hubris is that people believe they're in the know completely.[41]

What are the unnamed elephants that get in the way of creating cultures that nurture respectful, inclusive dialogue? We'll put it bluntly: We believe they are arrogance, hubris and aggressive leadership. Naming elephants and sharing ideas take courage. Aggressive, arrogant leaders create cultures in which some employees replicate the aggressive, arrogant behavior while others become passive. Marginal and powerless employees learn very quickly that it is better to do nothing than to do anything that will place them in the sight of an aggressive manager.

While dissecting the implosion of such companies as Enron, Global Crossing and Tyco, we read about a new norm of aggressive, arrogant leadership, sometimes called the *corporate aristocracy.* There is a very fine line between confidence and arrogance, and in yet another example of the normalization of deviance, we believe this line has moved in the last two decades. **We want to make explicit just how arrogance, hubris and screamers negatively impact organizations.**

How and why has the line between confidence and arrogance moved in the past two decades? Based on our research and experience we believe it is due to multiple factors, but

Hubris (n): exaggerated pride or self-confidence often resulting in retribution.[38]

Arrogance (n): offensive display of superiority or self-importance.[39]

Screamer (n): one who screams.[40]

53

we think three are significant.[42] Success is one factor, the "normalization of arrogance" is another, and the rise of the "Smart-Talk Trap"[43] is a third.

FIRST, SUCCESS BREEDS HUBRIS

*a*s we pointed out in the last chapter, the more success a group has, the less chance they will question their assumptions and be open to looking for changes in the environment. There is nothing like success to breed arrogance and a belief that it was all due to one's brilliance (hubris). That is, of course, until something — often unexpected because people are not looking for inconsistencies — happens to derail success. Then it becomes someone else's fault (the economy, the regulatory environment, unfair trade practices, the media, and even the weather).[44] For example, the former CEO of Enron, Jeff Skilling, maintained that Enron's demise came about because the banks called in their loans![45]

54

Xerox Corporation exhibited a typical case of organizational hubris. They were right to be proud of their brilliance as innovators. The Palo Alto Research Center (PARC) invented much of the technology later used to create personal computers, although Xerox didn't realize the commercial potential of most of it. One discovery did lead to the invention of copiers, and while protected under U.S. patent law, Xerox essentially created and owned the market. However, as the sales poured in, the organization created a bureaucracy to manage the money. That bureaucracy began to believe that Xerox's success was due to its brilliance in management and superior selling skills rather than innovative research. The research culture transitioned into a culture focused on maintaining bureaucratic systems. The company's pride in the sales results of its innovative products became exaggerated confidence (hubris) in its genius for sales. Convinced the company was just as good at selling as inventing, Xerox even packaged and sold its selling skills as a training program.

Unfortunately, once the patent expired, the competitive environment proved that Xerox's success was due to the luck of a monopoly. The company lost market share as fast as the Japanese firms could make sales calls. The Japanese firms actually sold copiers at a lower price than Xerox's manufacturing cost. By 1982, the 95 percent share Xerox had of the copier market was down to 13 percent.[46]

55

SECOND, THE NORMALIZATION OF ARROGANCE

Unlike an earlier time in our history when public servants, religious leaders, military leaders and astronauts were heroes, in the Eighties and Nineties, our heroes became people who made fortunes. In 1987, the movie *Wall Street* introduced the character Gordon Gecko, presumably based on Ivan Boesky,

"Little by little, the look of the country changes because of the men we admire."[47]

and his infamous statement "Greed is good"[48] — a sentiment some believe summarizes the last two decades. Like Gecko, many of these new heroes were arrogant and certain they were "in the know completely." **Arrogant people at the top of organizations make it almost impossible to create an atmosphere where lower-level people question the assumptions behind decisions or bring up bad news.**

In the face of arrogance, people become passive followers. They are especially reluctant to speak up when they are afraid it will lead to public humiliation by another type of arrogant manager, the Screamer. The Screamer literally screams at people in an effort to intimidate, to control others, or to make him or herself look more important. In emotional-intelligence terms, the Screamer does not know how to self-regulate. It is especially important for a Screamer to maintain control because "to him losing a little control is the same as losing total control."[49] Healthy organizations will not tolerate Screamers, but arrogant, aggressive organizations tend to recruit and accept them, especially when they deliver results. The research and understanding of the concept of emotional intelligence have increased substantially in the last 10 years, but arrogant leaders have always been around. Before emotional intelligence was well-known, Harry Levinson discussed the concept in a *Harvard Business Review* article entitled, "The Abrasive Personality."[50] He describes these personality types as generally extremely talented and smart individuals who seem to know who they have to charm (up) and who they can bully (down). Most important, they tend to deliver an important service or set of results to the company. They "get the numbers." **Abrasive managers believe they can do what they want because the company cannot get along without them. While many don't survive over the long term, the damage they do during their tenure substantially undermines whatever results they deliver in the short run.** The business press is full of stories about abrasive leaders, although these corporate bullies create so much fear it's very difficult to get anyone to talk on the record even after they are gone.

the interesting thread through all the stories about abrasive managers is their vein of brilliance. They are very good at what they do — up to a point. They are often the hardest workers and say things like "I don't ask anything of others that I won't do." If they are lucky, they get a good mentor or coach early on who convinces them to change their style. *Fortune* described this in an article entitled "Get over Yourself: Your Ego Is out of Control."[51] One executive was devastated when his boss told him people couldn't stand working with him. He had to learn to listen and monitor where he stood on the confidence/arrogance line, especially when he was under stress. Those who don't get or

57

hear this feedback not only derail their own careers, they also may take down the company.

for example, Warnaco's Linda Wachner was reportedly an abrasive manager. She was given credit for building Warnaco from "a sleepy bra company with $590 million in sales into a $2.25 billion-a-year powerhouse. However, she also developed a reputation for demoralizing employees by publicly dressing them down for missing sales and profit goals or for simply displeasing her."[52] The first consequence of the over-controlling, abrasive manager is that high performers who have a choice of getting a job elsewhere, leave as soon as they can, stripping the organization of a lot of talent. One former Warnaco executive explains it this way: "She [Wachner] is the main reason why Warnaco has grown and the main reason it has fallen apart. There is some genius there, but she cannot run a $2 billion corporation by herself."[53]

58

By early 2001, the company had collapsed. By then Warnaco was being investigated by the SEC and dealing with several class-action lawsuits by shareholders "contending that Warnaco and its executives artificially inflated the price of the company's stock by issuing false and misleading statements about its financial performance."[54] Wachner was fired in November, 2001, just five months after Warnaco filed for bankruptcy protection. To anyone who has read the paper in the last two years, that sounds remarkably like another very public example of corporate hubris, Enron.

because Enron had such an arrogant culture, we would bet there were lots of Screamers. We know of at least one, and the damage he caused is the stuff of corporate legend. According to many published reports, Andrew Fastow, the former CFO of Enron, was also a master at intimidation. Smith and Emshwiller, authors of *24 Days*, describe him this way:

"Fastow also had a reputation as a screamer, who negotiated by intimidation and tirade. An official at one major bank recalled getting awakened at 2:00 a.m. by a shouting Fastow who was unhappy about the pace of a particular loan transaction. 'He would call you an idiot, though in more colorful language,' said the banker. 'Then the next day you'd talk to him and he would apologize profusely. It was all part of his persona. Charm and brimstone.'"[55]

Fastow survived and prospered because he delivered the numbers to an organization that valued meeting financial objectives above all else. But it wasn't just Fastow. Wall Street and the business press also lauded Enron's CEO, Jeff Skilling while he delivered the numbers. While Enron was making money, people "admired" the extremely arrogant culture Skilling set out to create at Enron. Enron's culture is also an

59

example of one of the trends we believe contributed to the normalization of arrogance, the rise of the "Smart-Talk Trap."

THIRD, THE SMART-TALK TRAP

Stanford University professors Jeffrey Pfeffer and Robert Sutton write that the smart talk trap is created when "leadership potential is equated with the ability to speak intelligently and often,"[56] and where talk becomes a substitute for action or execution. They explain that smart talk also has a negative aspect:

"We found that a particular kind of talk is an especially insidious inhibitor of organizational action: 'smart talk.' The elements of smart talk include sounding confident, articulate, and eloquent; having interesting information and ideas; and possessing a good vocabulary. But smart talk tends to have other, less benign components: first, it focuses on the negative, and second, it is unnecessarily complicated or abstract (or both). ...But the more negative components of smart talk, the tendency to tear an idea down without offering anything positive in its place and the belief that complex language and ideas are somehow better than simple ones — cannot be rationalized so easily."[57]

Tearing down an idea without offering anything positive in its place is the opposite of constructive dialogue. Talking in overly complex language and creating perfect plans have become substitutes for action in some organizations. Pfeffer and Sutton blame the rise in smart talk on the business school education model that rewards the ability to speak rather than the actual execution of ideas. For example, they contrast how medical schools expect students to learn by "hearing one, seeing one, doing one." For business students, law students and other professional graduate school students, the emphasis is typically on talk because the product or service is produced by talk. The way you debate ideas in order to pool knowledge to create a better product can be either constructive or destructive. Oppositional language, personal attacks and "criticism for criticism's sake"[58] is destructive. Using overly complex language and buzzwords confuses and intimidates people. Those who don't understand the terms stay quiet in order to not look stupid. People may leave the debate with little understanding of what they are supposed to do. Thus the trap closes and execution is lost while people try to figure out what is going on. They become passive and choose not to do anything rather than risk making a mistake.

61

the reason the smart talk trap has had such a large impact on organizational cultures also reflects the context of the past two decades. The Eighties represent the real beginning of the global economy, the Internet and the increased complexity (and velocity) of running a business. Organizations hired large numbers of highly educated people, many trained in smart talk, to manage the complexity. At the same time, the nature of work in organizations changed from employees operating machines to employees pooling their knowledge to create products. Obviously, knowledge workers have to share what they know in order for the organization to use it to create a service. Talk became the way we worked. Yet, most organizations did not explicitly address the competency of how to talk productively.

american businesses found they had to rely on relationships and constructive conversations at the very same time they had hired people who had learned that the way to get ahead was to sound smart by speaking often and in complex language. The wise organizations stopped, surfaced their assumptions about how people should work (and talk) together, given the new demands of the workplace. Others just behaved as they had in the old, machine-based economy. Enron did both.

62

When you read the books and stories about Enron, it's clear that Jeff Skilling was talented. Skilling questioned the long-held assumptions of the energy industry that believed hard assets were the most important assets. He turned this upside down to a groundbreaking and lucrative short-term result. However, once success occurred, Skilling stopped the process by not questioning his own assumptions and not allowing others to question him. He divided the world into those who "get it," which meant those who saw things as he did, and those that he felt were resisting the new way.

by creating only two categories of people, Skilling cultivated a culture that was not open to new information or unexpected results. A clear product of his time, Skilling also "believed that greed was the greatest motivator, and he was only too happy to feed it."[59] He hired many highly educated people and he expected them to fight with their peers for recognition and rewards. He thought that a certain level of tension between people was good because it fostered creativity. Unfortunately, because of the systems Enron adopted, that tension was diverted to gaining monetary rewards instead of executing better business results.

Many first-rate people with good intentions worked hard at Enron. With those resources it should have been a long-term success. However, the systems and arrogant leadership created a culture that rewarded "corporate killers where money seemed to be the only thing that mattered. Gradually people who prized teamwork were weeded out by the process, and those who stayed and thrived were the ones who were the most ruthless in cutting deals and looking out for themselves."[60] The result was that fewer people spoke up, information was hoarded, bad news was hidden and ultimately laws were broken. The price of passivity included bringing down

63

an accounting firm (although the book *24 Days* explores how Arthur Andersen's arrogant culture contributed to its downfall), implicating several major financial firms in criminal activity, and causing thousands of innocent people to lose their jobs and their savings. While we'd like to think Enron was unique, it is only exceptional in the scale of the consequences of its aggressive/passive culture.

WHAT CAN YOU DO?

Chances are you will find yourself working in an aggressive culture or dealing with an arrogant manager at some point in your career, if not now. Or you may have crossed the confidence/arrogance line yourself. We hope that by now, you're convinced that arrogance makes constructive dialogue impossible. What can you do?

THE INTENT/IMPACT GAP

One of the first things you can do is to become aware of how your intent differs from your actual impact on others. This is the individual application of the saying/doing gap. With the widespread use of 360-Degree Feedback instruments, many leaders can get information on how their actions are perceived by others.[61] Remember, people see your actions through their particular filters. The impact your behavior has on others might not match your intent. For example, a leader who asks his employees a lot of questions may intend to mentor his employees; his employees may experience it as micro-managing. A leader who pushes her team to constantly reassess their decisions may intend to inspire the group to creative breakthroughs. Her group may experience it as an indication they can't ever do enough to make their boss happy. When leaders receive feedback on how their behavior actually impacts their employees, they are often shocked. "But I didn't intend to send the message that I didn't trust them," they wail. "Why do my employees feel this way?" Multiple realities strike again.

Like organizations, individuals have to become inquisitive to a fault about how they are perceived by others. This is helped by acknowledging there are other valid views and being open to their influence. It is the opposite of smart talk. You may not even realize that you have shut down to alternative views or facts that don't fit your case. But people around you do. If their ideas aren't listened to, people stop offering them.

We think that all of the arrogant leaders we've profiled truly believed that what they were doing would have a positive impact on their organizations. We don't think any of them had malicious intent. However, they thought they knew best and had initial success. Success fueled arrogance to the point of hubris. When their organizations began to falter, it was a surprise to them. Instead of trying alternative behaviors or being open to new information, they did more of the same.

While acknowledging this is important for all levels, Tops have to pay special attention because people are very careful about what they tell the Tops. A colleague asked her boss (the CEO) pointedly, "Do you want me to tell you what I think or what I think you want to hear?" The CEO was offended. He was unaware of the impact of his behavior and that the information he received was filtered and parsed. It takes courage to even ask this question and our colleague was not rewarded. She was labeled "not a team player" and she finally left the company in frustration. Successful people will tell you that you don't get promoted if you don't have an ego. However, leaders at any level will also tell you to make sure you have people around who will challenge you. These employees don't challenge you to trap you in smart talk. Instead they understand that the purpose of the conversation is to uncover new data for better decision-making. The goal is to beat the external competition, not each other.

There are many other leadership strategies to employ and there are many good books that describe them in detail. However, leadership ultimately comes down to conversations and connections; asking questions; listening to responses; and ensuring that impact matches intent.

In the next chapter, we offer specific strategies to use to name elephants and to encourage others to do so.

!

CONVERSATION STARTERS

- How successful do we think we have been? Have we morphed into hubris?
- Has our success blinded us to questioning our assumptions?
- How have we dealt with abrasive managers? What message does this send?
- Have we fallen into the smart talk trap, where we reward those who attack others' ideas but who offer no positive alternatives?
- Have we embraced complex buzzwords with no apparent value added?
- What three words would customers use to describe our organization?
- How do I know if my impact matches my intent?

!

EXAMPLES OF THE SAYING/DOING GAP AT ENRON[62]

- *What they said they believed*
  We do not tolerate abusive or disrespectful treatment.
- *How they behaved*
  Those who make money for Enron can be abusive and disrespectful.

- *What they said they believed*
  Ruthlessness, callousness and arrogance don't belong here.
- *How they behaved*
  Being ruthless, callous and arrogant is expected from smart people.

- *What they said they believed*
  We work with customers and prospects openly, honestly and sincerely.
- *How they behaved*
  We will take advantage of every customer and prospect in order to win.

69

- *What they said they believed*
  When we say we will do something, we will do it; when we say we cannot or will not do something, then we won't do it.
- *How they behaved*
  It doesn't matter what we said yesterday; what do we need to do today to get our numbers?

- *What they said they believed*
  Here, we have to take the time to talk with one another ... and to listen.
- *How they behaved*
  Deals are the only things that matter; if you have to walk over someone else, do it.

- *What they said they believed*
  We are satisfied with nothing less than the very best in everything we do.
- *How they behaved*
  It doesn't matter how we execute as long as we make money.

- *What they said they believed*
  The great fun here will be for all of us to discover
  just how good we can really be.
- *How they behaved*
  The great fun here will be to see how much money
  I can make.

CHAPTER FOUR

Strategies to Encourage the Naming of Elephants

What was rarely stated aloud, but what most people in the company knew, was that the trouble spot was located in Enron Capital & Trade, Jeff Skilling's creation.[63]

Both Columbia and Challenger were lost also because of the failure of NASA's organizational system .... Management did not listen to what their engineers were telling them.[64]

et's be frank. Naming elephants can be dangerous to your career. As he reflected on an opportunity to name an elephant, a client recently told us, "I would have been fired if I had spoken up." Others have said something like this: "I don't get paid enough money to take the risk. Let the Tops who make the big bucks take the responsibility." The risk of naming elephants is real. However, the risk of not naming elephants also carries a price — for you and the organization. How do you question the status quo and come out a hero rather than a villain? The goal of this chapter is to give you specific strategies for assessing and dealing with the risk.[65]

IF ONLY THEY WOULD CHANGE

Southwest Airlines gives out a button that shows "They" with a red slash through it. It is a reminder to employees that there is no "they." We agree with Southwest's explicit emphasis on the value and power of each person to change an organization. Yes, you are part of a system, and the system does determine to

73

some extent how you behave, but you also shape the system by your behavior. We tell our clients, you can only start with you. You can't really change your boss or your peers, but you can change the questions you ask, who you ask and how you react when you hear unexpected results. However, in our work with organizations, we see a lot of finger-pointing and "if only they would change" excuses. In one dramatic example, we watched a group of 1,800 people answer the following questions with a hand-held voting device:

- Does your boss need to change?
- Do your peers need to change?
- Do your subordinates need to change?
- Do you need to change?

the results were consistent and came up on an instant graph. Eighty percent agreed that the boss, their peers and their subordinates needed to change. Only 20 percent thought they needed to change. Of course they were sitting with their peers, their bosses and some subordinates, so the numbers did not add up. However, this is typical. The two widespread assumptions operating in many organizations are that everyone but me needs to change, and that one person cannot possibly make a difference. We simply do not agree. Every organization change effort succeeds only if individuals alter their behavior. Because everyone in an organization actually works in relationship with someone else, one person's

74

change affects another person and eventually the numbers begin to add up to create the tipping point or a critical mass.

What can you do differently today? We divided these strategies into three categories: what you as an individual can do; what you as an individual need to remember when you listen to others; and, what you can do as the leader of a work group to encourage the naming of elephants. We invite you to stay in the spirit of our first suggestion: Start small. The organization may be the five people you work with.

!

INDIVIDUAL STRATEGIES TO NAME ELEPHANTS

START SMALL

The actual skill of naming elephants is quite simple to learn. However, like most skills, you will want to practice when the stakes are low. Begin by asking the following questions at the end of each meeting you attend: What is the unnamed elephant in this room and what do we need to do about it? As people become more comfortable with the actual process and begin to share a common language, they will be more willing to speak up when the stakes are higher.

75

PAY ATTENTION TO "LEEMERS"

We love this term. It is the word used by naval aviators to express their gut feeling that something is wrong even if they can't quite put their finger on what it is. Weick and Sutcliffe speculate that it comes from the word leery (wary, suspicious).[66] When you consider how quickly a pilot has to react if something goes wrong, you can understand why he or she pays attention as soon as he senses a leemer. The gut feeling is an early warning system that may put you on the trail of achieving great success or avoiding a costly failure.

CREATE CROSS-CHECKS

We've all heard flight attendants announce this term over the intercom. When the aircraft doors are closed at departure time, the flight attendants arm the doors so that in an emergency the slides will automatically inflate. When the plane lands, the first thing the flight attendants do is disarm the doors. They announce to each other that the cross-check has occurred so the door can be opened safely.[67] The way you can use cross-checks is to ask someone to play devil's advocate to your thinking and decision-making processes. Think out loud and ask them to tell you what information or view you might be blind to. Just don't get defensive when someone offers you an opinion. Envision the consequences of a slide

76

inflating at O'Hare during the busiest departure/arrival time and you can see the benefit of using cross-checks.

AVOID THE BLAME GAME

You may for example, think the unnamed elephant is a leadership mistake. Perhaps you think your boss made a bad decision. We do not recommend barging into his or her office, waving this book, telling him or her you think the unnamed elephant is their incompetence. Go back and figure out how you participated (or didn't participate) in the decision. What was the impact of your action or inaction? Maybe you had doubts but didn't speak up at the time. Perhaps you now realize you had a completely different set of assumptions from your boss and you never compared them. Identify your contribution to the situation and begin the conversation with that.[68]

!

STRATEGIES TO ENCOURAGE OTHERS TO NAME ELEPHANTS

UNDERSTAND THE VALUE OF RELATIONSHIPS

employees need to trust that their ideas will be valued and not belittled or dismissed. Building trust is only done through relationships and relationships take time. In their book *Execution*, Larry Bossidy and Ram Charan estimate that 40 percent of an effective leader's time is spent on people issues. They point out that: "This immense personal commitment is time-consuming and fraught with emotional wear and tear in giving feedback, conducting dialogues, and exposing your judgment to others. But the foundation of a great company is the way it develops people."[69] There are no shortcuts in developing people, but here are some time-stretching suggestions.

- Change the way you hold meetings and take turns to allow everyone to speak. This creates opportunities for people to build relationships and sends the message that you want to hear what others think. Consider rotating the leadership responsibility for the meeting among your employees.
- Instead of hitting the seductive reply button on your email, walk to the person's desk if possible. Face-to-face interaction builds relationships and may also cue you into subtle signals of concern that

are missing in emails.

- Return phone calls in the shortest period of time possible without regard to the perceived status and rank of the caller. Failure to return phone calls in a timely manner (or at all) creates a lot of anger in the corporate world. Remember that all members of your organization have something valuable to offer.

- Host an informal lunch on a regularly scheduled basis. Order pizza or sandwiches if the budget allows and keep it to 30 minutes. Ask everyone to share an idea — about something they learned in the last week as the "price" of lunch. Or just use the time for informal conversation so people can get to know each other — and you — better.

DEFAULT TO THE CURIOUS, NOT THE DEFENSIVE

If we hear someone else name an elephant we weren't ready to discuss, we generally default to the defensive. This is where it pays to be aware of your intent/impact gap. Do you immediately react in a manner that shuts others down? Take a deep breath and get curious. Ask the following questions:

- What are our differing assumptions?

- When did we last debate the relevancy of these assumptions?
- What new evidence have we uncovered that may challenge these assumptions?
- How can we make sure we have asked the right people how they see the situation?
- What are our next steps?
- Use "how can we do that" type questions rather than the defensiveness-producing "why should we do that."

LISTEN/BE OPEN TO NEW IDEAS

this seems so obvious, yet in our organizational consulting practice we have found a widespread perception that "they" — meaning Middles and Tops — aren't open or listening to new ideas. People who become Middles or Tops are talented and good at seeing what needs to be done, and they can be counted on to execute. However, in order to stay successful, Middles and Tops also need the ideas and knowledge of the people who work for them. There really isn't any organization that can afford to waste employees by not accessing what they know. To do that, everyone has to start to listen and be open to new ideas, or ways of looking at data. If you even suspect your employees think you're not listening, get some coaching. A good coach can positively increase your impact in this area in a relatively short period of time.

NO NEWS IS BAD NEWS

1 n direct contrast to the former widespread assumption that no news is good news, the opposite is true. Perhaps the messenger has been shot too many times in the past. Perhaps arrogant leadership has created passive employees hiding in their cubes. In an organization that relies on the assets in people's heads, you have to know what people know. If it's too quiet, go out and start asking people what's happening. Use constructive dialogue techniques to get some conversation going. Expect the unexpected and use it to be ready before your competition. Put what Jim Collins calls "catalytic mechanisms" in place. For example, while he was a business-school professor, he gave each of his students a sheet of red paper to use as a "red flag" anytime during the semester. If a student held up the red flag, the entire class had to stop and pay attention to that student. Catalytic mechanisms even out the power and status issues and give everyone a chance to speak up, thus ensuring Collins would hear from all students at least once in the semester.[70]

DEALING WITH ARROGANCE

dealing with an insufferably arrogant person is emotionally taxing, but because the line between confidence and arrogance is so thin, chances are you will have to deal with arrogance on a semi-regular basis. Confident people are generally curious, so try to engage the curiosity of the arrogant person. Perhaps he or she has just crossed over that fine line for a moment and you can bring him or her back with your questions. Another strategy is to remember that arrogance is often a cover for insecurity. That may help you keep it in perspective and realize that insecure people fear losing control. At the very least, make it your goal to learn something from this person. Even if you only discover what he or she is most worried about, you can probably put that information to use with more reasonable people.

!

LEADERSHIP STRATEGIES TO PROMOTE THE NAMING OF ELEPHANTS

INSTITUTE A NAME-THE-ELEPHANT AWARD

to create a comfort zone around naming elephants, have some fun with the metaphor. Institute an award for the best-named elephant of the week. Elevate people who bring in ideas, new evidence, and new ways of seeing; make them into heroes rather than villains. We want to emphasize that you can do this in your work group without waiting for an organization-wide initiative.

ESTABLISH AN OMBUDSMAN ROLE

An ombudsman[71] can play the role of data gatherer and identifier of elephants. The keys to a successful ombudsman position are independence from the traditional hierarchy, neutrality and confidentiality. This role traditionally is a resource for employees and senior management to open up the lines of communication and resolve issues — individual and systemic — before they become too large to handle in an informal manner.

CREATE A NAMING ELEPHANT WEBSITE

Many large organizations already have websites where people go to "talk." These are the electronic water coolers we referred to before. Some are company-sponsored, others are not. The wise Top finds his or her way to those websites to listen and respond to what people talk about without punishing those who name elephants.

USE THE POWER OF A "FUNDAMENTAL SURPRISE"[72]

September 11, 2001, was an example of a fundamental surprise. It called for a review of many of our assumptions. Unimagined before it happened, we now try to make sense of why we didn't anticipate it. Our human tendency is to try to place blame. Instead, the fundamental surprise should be an opportunity to review and reexamine the system, our assumptions and choices. It is also an opportunity to grow. Realize that the window for motivating people to change is relatively short because people will make the shifts in their assumptions and then go on with life. That can result in what Paul Romer calls a waste of a crisis. The question every person should ask is, what have we learned, and more importantly, what are we doing differently as a result of the fundamental surprise?

REVISE AND REASSESS

Build scheduled time into any project to stop and reassess the current situation. The goal should be to look for new information and assess if the assumptions used to make the decisions on the project are still valid. For example, when

Coca-Cola introduced New Coke and faced an immediate customer revolt, it would have been easy to dismiss it as temporary. After all, the company had spent three years researching consumer tastes. It had based New Coke's formula on the assumption that customers' tastes had changed to prefer a sweeter formula. When Coke reexamined how it had come to that conclusion, the company realized its research process had been flawed. Coke set a short deadline for a decision and during that time stayed open to all new information. Less than three months after the product launch it re-released the old Coke as Coke Classic. Coke isn't known as a particularly humble organization, but in this case it actually admitted it made a mistake. As a result, customers felt they had been listened to, and Coke didn't suffer any long-term consequences.

DON'T DRIFT INTO HUBRIS

taking time to celebrate success is an important organizational ritual. However, remember the fine line between confidence and arrogance. You have to be confident to lead an organization, but arrogance will create many blocks to learning. Monitor your reactions when you hear something that disturbs your worldview; this may be an early warning that you're drifting into hubris. Ask yourself what you learned today and from whom. If you find you are only learning from the same short list of names, you may need to expand your circle.

85

ASSUME INCOMPLETE COMMUNICATION

One of the sidebars in the CAIB addresses the flaws of compressing complex information into PowerPoint presentations. The demand for formal, succinct executive summaries may blind decision-makers to unnamed elephants. Email adds to this because the human face is missing. There is no shortcut to the human process of communication. If you don't have the time, ask yourself what it would take for you to have the time. After an accident or organizational failure, there always seems to be plenty of time for inquiry. Why not invest it upfront? Ask yourself, who should we talk to that we haven't talked to? Review what status and power issues might be getting in the way of communication. Think about who has spoken up and who hasn't and ask yourself why.

EXPLORE THE SAYING/DOING GAPS

When one of our client companies had a serious financial setback; it realized it had to quickly make expense control a key value. A tiger team was created to find ways to cut expenses. This team soon realized that expense control had to apply equally to the Tops, Middles and Bottoms. They had the difficult task of telling the Tops that their perks of first-class air travel, limo service to the airport and executive dining privileges had to go. This organization's leader agreed and set the example. Remember, people believe what you do, not what you say. If the rules don't apply to the Tops, you will breed cynicism.

LEARN FROM YOUR SUCCESS

We've cited lessons from some failures in this book, but we also want to encourage you to learn from your successes. Take the time to name the elephant, surface assumptions and have constructive dialogue about things you do well as an organization. (See one of our other books, *The Thin Book of®Appreciative Inquiry*, for more on how to do this). Assume you have examples of extraordinary performance and find them and learn from them. The fact that the positive examples are within your organization may give you even more relevant data for future application.

THE REAL PRICE OF PASSIVITY: LOSING OPPORTUNITY

Throughout this book, we have written about the risk of not listening. If a leader is perceived as not being open to new ideas and not listening, we can all but guarantee there are opinions and ideas that she needs in order to be successful that she is not getting. The lesson for all of us is that no matter how skilled we are individually at guiding an organization, if we are missing ideas, opinions and new directions, we are jeopardizing ultimate individual and organizational success. The risk of missing opportunity is the Price of Passivity for most organizations. Passive people won't execute. They will find corners of the organization in which to hide. It takes attention to create a different culture. You can begin by bringing a relentless curiosity to your organization. Ask the tough questions. *What information might I not be getting? What are the consequences of that?* And then push further by asking the following:

- What do you say you believe? Contrast that with your actual behaviors.
- How do the Tops, Middles and Bottoms behave in your organization? Contrast the differences. (Are the Tops served coffee at their meetings, while the Bottoms have to buy theirs?)
- How do you know what you know and what you don't know?
- What kind of "fights" do you have?
- How do you ensure the Bottoms actually speak and are heard?
- How do you explicitly deal with power and status differentials?
- How do you deal with arrogance?
- Name three things that keeps any organizational member awake at night.

every person impacts a culture by the questions he or she asks and the type of conversations he or she has. It only takes one brave person to bring up the undiscussables or name the elephant. We can't stress enough that it also can take only one leader to shut it down.

What You Can Do Today

There are over 6 billion voices around the world ...

Are you listening? [73]

W e admit it is uncomfortable to disturb the status quo. However, we hope this book has disturbed yours in a constructive way. We truly believe that **organizational change begins with you. If you don't have the authority to make the decisions, you certainly have the authority to challenge the decisions.** If you are a member of an organization, you have the responsibility to be mindful, to push back, to name elephants, and to add your "sense" to the group. If you are a leader, you also have the responsibility to create a culture in which all employees can contribute fully to the organization.

We work with some clients who are trying to do that. The client referenced in the introduction is making progress: Revenues are up and expenses down. We were very happy to hear a key group of Middles tell us recently that they now believe they can make a difference without waiting for the Tops to change. This client is well on the way to eliminating the "they."

We know that NASA is hard at work on its culture change. Its public documents state that NASA has set a goal of agency-wide culture transformation with a focus on safety excellence.

The agency's goal is to once again become a High Reliability Organization.[74]

*g*oing back to basics has helped us be more effective too. We used the language in this book with a new client recently and he realized that he had to name an elephant in his organization. He created a PowerPoint presentation to explain to his staff in his own words what that meant. For the first time, he is also trying to create open dialogue with his group. While this is a relatively small change within a large organization, he reports it will save significant money and time. As consultants, we count this as a success because we were able to transfer the skills to him and he feels comfortable and motivated to do this work without us.

THREE UNIVERSAL HUMAN NEEDS

We conclude with what we believe is the most powerful guide to creating an organizational culture that will nurture open, inclusive dialogue. It is the practice of recognizing and respecting the three universal human needs. You can incorporate these into your leadership practices no matter what kind of environment you currently work in because they involve how you treat each individual. Several management theorists have articulated the three universal human needs although in different forms. We cite David Cooperrider's[75] version. He believes that each person has the need to:

91

- Have a voice and be heard;
- Be viewed as essential to a group; and
- Be seen as unique and exceptional.

We have found that when people in organizations become frustrated or cynical, it is always because the organization is not fully respectful of the three universal human needs. In our experience, most organizations will tell you they practice these principles, but in reality they do not. They are deceptively simple. You can make a difference by monitoring who you listen to and who you ignore and asking yourself why. What assumptions have you made about people or their positions that cause you to listen or tune out?

You can make a difference in creating a more constructive culture at your organization by:

- Being curious about how every other person sees the world;
- Respecting each person's perspective of the world as unique and essential to the group's success; and
- Making sure every person has a chance to speak and be heard.

Ultimately, if you ensure all three needs are met, you will be successful as a leader. If your organization works at meeting all three needs, your organization will be more successful. You never know when the voice with the million-dollar idea will speak up, so be sure to listen. **We invite you to share your stories with us and with others at our website, www.nametheelephant.com.**

Endnotes

[1] Theodore Roosevelt, <u>An Autobiography</u>, paperback edition (Da Capo Press, 1985) p. 209. We are indebted to Smith & Emshwiller for bringing this wonderful quote to our attention.

[2] Thomas Friedman, "Kicking over the Chessboard," <u>New York Times</u> (4/18/2004) p.13.

[3] You can read this report on the website www.caib.us/news/report. Our quoted points are from pp. 97 & 177.

[4] Chris Argyris termed the two 'espoused theory' and 'theory-in use' in the 1970s.

[5] Karl Weick, Kathleen Sutcliffe, <u>Managing the Unexpected</u> (John Wiley & Sons, 2001) p. 46.

[6] Diane Vaughan, <u>The Challenger Launch Decision</u> (The University of Chicago Press, 1996).

[7] CAIB, p. 149.

[8] Also see an excellent article written at the time we were working on this book. Richard Mason, "Lessons in Organizational Ethics from the *Columbia* Disaster," <u>Organizational Dynamics</u> (33:2, 2004) pp. 128-142. We read and cite many of the same books and articles but Dr. Mason explains more about organizational culture and ethics.

[9] Claudia Dreifus, "Painful Questions from an Ex-Astronaut," <u>New York Times</u>, (8/26/03) p. D2.

[10] Ibid.

[11] Millions of school children were scheduled to watch the *Challenger* launch because of teacher turned astronaut, Christa McAuliffe.

[12] There actually had been a close call in 1988. See William Langewiesche's article on *"Columbia's* Last Flight" or the CAIB report, Chapter 6.

[13] William Langewiesche, *"Columbia's* Last Flight," The Atlantic Monthly, (November, 2003) p. 35 on www.theatlantic.com.

[14] Ibid. This is a must-read article! This quote is from page 37 of the copy of the article on www.theatlantic.com.

[15] Barry Oshry, Seeing Systems: Unlocking the Mysteries of Organizational Life. (Berrett–Koehler Publishers, 1995) p.xiii.

[16] CAIB, p. 177.

[17] Chris Argyris, "Skilled Incompetence," Managing with People in Mind (Harvard Business Review Press paperback No. 90085).

[18] Ken, Yamada, "Grove's Network Computer View," Computer Reseller News (10/28/1996).

[19] See Good To Great (Harper Business, 2001) by Jim Collins for more on how good companies become great by doing this.

[20] These norms are based on our conjecture. See the CAIB and NASA's website for the Assessment and Plan for Organizational Culture Change at NASA (3/15/04) www.nasa.gov/about/highlights/culture_survey.html.

[21] Karlene Kerfoot, "Attending to Weak Signals: The Leader's Challenge," Nursing Economics (11/1/2003).

[22] Webster's 7th Collegiate Dictionary (1973), p. 419.

[23] Webster's New Unabridged Dictionary (2003), p. 681.

Endnotes

[24] Our colleague James Powers told us that when he began consulting in the 60s, the expression was "there is a dead body on the table and it will soon begin to smell unless we acknowledge and talk about it."

[25] Jerry Harvey, "The Abilene Paradox: The Management of Agreement." Organizational Dynamics (Summer 1974) pp. 63-80.

[26] Doug Stone, Bruce Patton, Sheila Heen, Difficult Conversations (Penguin Books, 1999), Susan Scott, Fierce Conversations (Viking Books, 2002).

[27] David Halberstam, The Reckoning (William Morrow & Co, 1986).

[28] Micheline Maynard, The End of Detroit (Currency, 2003).

[29] And some great books with good descriptions of the process. See the Resource section.

[30] James F. Short, Jr. "Social Organization and Risk: Some Current Controversies." Annual Review of Sociology (1/1/1993).

[31] Weick, Sutcliffe, op. cit. We highly recommend this gem of a book.

[32] Karl Weick, "Prepare your Organization to Fight Fires," Harvard Business Review (May-June, 1996), Reprint 96311.

[33] Karl Weick, The Social Psychology of Organizing (Random House, 1969, 1979) p.6.

[34] Ibid. p.7.

[35] Jim Collins, Good To Great (Harper, 2001).

[36] Thanks to our colleague Mike O'Brien for his expertise in this area of corporate culture. See www.starpg.com.

[37] CAIB, p. 203.

[38] Webster's New Collegiate Dictionary, p. 556.

[39] Webster's Unabridged Dictionary, p. 116.

[40] Webster's New Collegiate Dictionary, p. 1038.

[41] K. Hammonds, K. Weick, "It Is a World after Enron," Fast Company (May 2002) pp. 126-128.

[42] Also see, Michael Maccoby, "Narcissistic Leaders: The Incredible Pros, the Inevitable Cons," Harvard Business Review (Jan, 2004) Reprint R0401J: HBR OnPoint 5904.

[43] Jeffrey Pfeffer, Robert Sutton, "The Smart-Talk Trap," Harvard Business Review (May-June 1999) Reprint 4061.

[44] See the classic article, Edward H. Bowman, "Strategy and the Weather," Sloan Management Review (Winter 1976) pp. 49-62.

[45] Bethany McLean, Peter Elkind, Smartest Guys in the Room (Penguin, 2003) p. 414.

[46] Business Week, "Xerox: The Downfall" (3/5/2001).

[47] Larry McMurtry, Hud (Popular Library, 1961).

[48] In 1985, Ivan Boesky actually said, "I think greed is healthy. You can be greedy and still feel good about yourself." (www.washingtonpost.com)

[49] Harry Levinson, "The Abrasive Personality," Harvard Business Review (May-June, 1978) p. 88.

[50] Levinson, H. op. cit.

97

Endnotes

[51] Fortune, "Get Over Yourself" (4/30/2001).

[52] Leslie Kaufman "Questions of Style in Warnaco's Fall," New York Times (5/6/2001).

[53] Ibid.

[54] Ibid.

[55] Rebecca Smith, John Emshwiller, 24 Days (Harper Business, 2003) p. 73.

[56] Pfeffer, Sutton, op. cit. p.136.

[57] Ibid. pp. 136, 138.

[58] Ibid. p. 134.

[59] McLean, Elkind, op. cit. p. 55.

[60] Ibid p. 121.

[61] For more on this process see The Thin Book of®360 Feedback: A Manager's Guide. www.thinbook.com.

[62] All espoused values are from Enron's 1998 Annual Report listed as "Our Values." The actual norms are our conjecture. See Smartest Guys in the Room, p. xix.

[63] Mimi Swartz, Sherron Watkins, Power Failure. (Doubleday, 2003) p.76.

[64] CAIB, pp.195, 201.

[65] Also see a very extensive treatment of how to become The Courageous Messenger by Kathleen Ryan, Daniel Oestreich, and George Orr (Jossey-Bass, 1996).

[66] Weick, Sutcliffe, op. cit. p. 41.

[67] We are grateful to our colleague, Kathleen Duffy for her help with this example.

[68] See <u>Difficult Conversation</u> authors Stone, Patton and Heen's website for a worksheet on preparing for this kind of conversation. www.triadcgi.com.

[69] Larry Bossidy, Ram Charan, <u>Execution</u> (Crown Business, 2002) p.118.

[70] Jim Collins, "Turning Goals into Results: The Power of Catalytic Mechanisms," <u>Harvard Business Review</u> (July-August 1999).

[71] See The Ombudsman Association for more information on Ombudsman: http://www.ombuds-toa.org/code_of_ethics.htm.

[72] David Woods, <u>Beyond Human Error</u>. See his website http://csel.eng.ohio-state.edu/woods for a fascinating discussion of this topic. His writing helped us understand many of the issues of HROs and NASA.

[73] From: http://iacs5.ucsd.edu/~mmogri/

[74] See David Wood's website for his testimony to Congress on NASA's progress.

[75] David Cooperrider, "Why Appreciative Inquiry," <u>Lessons from the Field: Applying Appreciative Inquiry</u> (Thin Book Publishing, 2002). Also see the work of David McClelland who identified three needs; achievement, affiliation, and power. Weick, (<u>Sensemaking</u>, p.21) also cites Erez and Earley's "three self-derived needs including a positive view of self, the desire to see oneself as competent and the need to experience coherence and continuity."

Acknowledgments

W e are extremely grateful to our readers who took the time to review drafts and give us honest feedback. Many of them wish to remain anonymous, but the following people agreed to be thanked in print: Carrie Coltman Arthur, Michelle L. Collins, Kathryn Gaulke, Mary C. Gushee, Barbara Hyder, Vonda K. Mills, Allison Gushee Molkenthin, Laura K. Moore, Thomas E. Stazyk, and Sandy Stubblefield. The final product should not in any way imply they approved it, but we hope they enjoy it. We could not have written this book without their generous gift of time.

We also wish to thank the colleagues who continue to teach us. They include James Powers, Michael O'Brien, Kathleen Duffy, Cathy Royal, and our brilliant partner, Michelle Collins. We want to protect the confidentially of our clients by not naming them. However, we appreciate that they continue to give us the opportunity to do what we love. We wish we could personally thank all the employees who, without hesitation, share their organizational experience with us. We learn a great deal from them.

Throughout the genesis of this book, Starbucks Store #602 at Lakeside Market in Plano, Texas, showed us repeatedly what a difference a great store manager makes in the life of her team and her customers. Janice and her staff inspired us and gave us the gift of a smile (and great coffee) on a daily basis.

finally, we wish to acknowledge our gratitude and dependence on the professors of organizational behavior who spend their lives studying organizations and freely sharing their wisdom. Chris Argyris, Donald Schon, Ed Schein, Peter Drucker, Marvin Weisbord and Karl Weick laid down the theory that most of the field relies on, almost 30 years ago. They and many others do the ongoing research to show us what we can count on and what we must question. In more recent years, Jerry Porras and Jim Collins have added a great deal of painstaking research and thought to the body of knowledge. John Slocum has spent his career translating complex concepts into plain English and has generously tutored Sue on the subject for over 12 years. We thank all of you for assisting us in our journey to better understand and serve organizations.

About the Authors

S ue Annis Hammond and Andrea B. Mayfield are partners with Michelle L. Collins in HRD Solutions (www.hrdsolutions.com). We offer pragmatic people development solutions to achieve individual, team and organizational success.

Sue Annis Hammond is a Change Management Consultant with a unique combination of extensive consulting and entrepreneurial experience. She has more than 20 years of consulting experience, including 10 years of internal work at two Fortune 500 companies, 12 years of external consulting, and six years as an entrepreneur.

Sue is a nationally recognized expert in Appreciative Inquiry, a process that changes the focus from finding out what is going wrong to discovering and expanding best practices in organizations. Her first book *The Thin Book of®Appreciative Inquiry* is a national bestseller, with sales in excess of 100,000 copies. Sue started Thin Book Publishing in response to the book's success and customer requests for more "thin books." The company is devoted to publishing 'just in time' cutting-edge knowledge for organizational clients.

Sue completed a Master's of Organizational Development at Bowling Green Graduate School of Business, where she was the 1991 Minninger Foundation Fellow. She also holds a B.A.

and M.A. in English from SUNY Fredonia, and currently lives in Bend, Oregon. She can be contacted at sue@hrdsolutions.com.

ndrea B. Mayfield is an Organization Development Consultant focused on leadership strategy work. With proven skills in leadership development, change management, and executive meeting facilitation, her principal focus is working with leaders to identify, plan and pursue development needs for themselves and their organizations. Her broad experience was developed through internal consulting work with NASA, American Airlines and Mary Kay Cosmetics as well as her external consulting practice. This combination of experiences has equipped her with an understanding of very large, complex organizations as well as fast-paced entrepreneurial settings.

Andrea's consulting services include confidential assistance in evaluating systems, designing strategies for change, and implementing interventions. She designs, manages and evaluates individual and system-wide leadership development programs. Andrea serves as an executive coach to executives in a variety of industries and has built high-potential development programs in large organizations.

Andrea has an Organization Development Certificate from Georgetown University, an M.A. in Community Counseling from the University of Maryland and a B.A. in Psychology from Dickinson College. Andrea currently resides in Coppell, Texas, and can be reached at andrea@hrdsolutions.com.

both Sue and Andrea offer workshops and keynote speeches on Naming the Elephant. For more information, visit our website, www.nametheelephant.com.

Resources

Argyris, Chris. "Skilled Incompetence". *Managing with People in Mind*. Harvard Business Review Press No. 90085. 1991.

Argyris, Chris and Schon, Donald. *Organizational Learning II*. Addison-Wesley, 1996.

Bohm, David. *On Dialogue*. Routledge,1996.

Bossidy, Larry and Charan, Ram. *Execution*. Crown Business, 2002.

Bowman, Edward H. "Strategy and the Weather". *Sloan Management Review*, Winter, 1976, pp.49-62.

BusinessWeek, "Xerox: The Downfall". March 5, 2001.

Collins, Jim. "Turning Goals into Results: The Power of Catalytic Mechanisms". *Harvard Business Review*. July-August, 1999.

Collins, Jim. *Good To Great*. Harper Business, 2001.

Columbia Accident Investigation Board: www.caib.us/news/report.

Resources

Cooperrider, David. "Why Appreciative Inquiry". *Lessons from the Field: Applying Appreciative Inquiry.* Thin Book Publishing, 2002.

Dreifus, Claudia. "Painful Questions from an Ex-Astronaut". *New York Times*, August 26, 2003.

Ellinor, Linda and Gerard, Glenna. *Dialogue.* John Wiley & Sons, 1998.

Erez, M. and Earley, P.C. *Culture, Self-Identity and Work.* Oxford University Press, 1993.

Friedman, Thomas. "Kicking over the Chessboard". *New York Times*, April 18, 2004, p. 13.

Gittell, J.H. *The Southwest Airlines Way.* McGrawHill, 2003.

Goleman, Daniel. "What Makes a Leader?" *Harvard Business Review*, 1998, reprint R0401H.

Goleman, Daniel. *Emotional Intelligence.* Bantam Books, 1995.

Halberstam, David. *The Reckoning.* William Morrow & Co, 1986.

Hammond, Sue A. *The Thin Book of® Appreciative Inquiry.* Thin Book Publishing Co, 1996, 1998.

Hammonds, K. and Weick, K. "It Is a World After Enron". *Fast Company*, May 2002, pp. 126-128.

Harvey, Jerry. "The Abilene Paradox: The Management of Agreement". *Organizational Dynamics*, Summer, 1974.

Kaufman, Leslie. "Questions of Style in Warnaco's Fall". *New York Times*, May 6, 2001.

Kerfoot, Karlene. "Attending to weak signals: The Leader's Challenge". *Nursing Economics*, November 1, 2003.

Langewiesche, William. Columbia's Last Flight. *The Atlantic Monthly*, November, 2003. www.theatlantic.com.

Levinson, Harry. "The Abrasive Personality". *Harvard Business Review*. May-June, 1978.

Maccoby, Michael. "Narcissistic Leaders: The Incredible Pros, the Inevitable Cons". *Harvard Business Review*. January, 2004. Reprint R0401J: HBR OnPoint 5904.

Maynard, Micheline. *The End of Detroit*. Currency, 2003.

Resources

Mason, Richard. "Lessons in Organizational Ethics from the Columbia Disaster". *Organizational Dynamics*, 33.2, 2004.

McClelland, David. *Human Motivation*. Scott, Foresman, 1985.

McLean, B. and Elkind, P. *The Smartest Guys in the Room*. Penguin Group, 2003.

McMurtry, Larry. *Hud*. Popular Library, 1961.

NASA: *Assessment and Plan for Organizational Culture Change at NASA*. March 15, 2004. www.nasa.gov/about/highlights/culture_survey.html.

Ombudsman Association, http://www.ombuds-toa.org/code_of_ethics.htm.

Oshry, Barry. *Seeing Systems: Unlocking the Mysteries of Organizational Life*. Berrett-Koehler Publishers, Inc., 1995, 1996.

Perrow, Charles. *Normal Accidents*. Princeton University Press, 1999.

Pfeffer, Jeffrey and Sutton, Robert. "The Smart-Talk Trap". *Harvard Business Review*. May-June, 1999. Reprint 4061.

Porras, J. and Collins. J. *Built To Last*. Harper Business, 1994.

Roosevelt, Theodore. *An Autobiography*. Charles Scribner's Sons, 1913. Da Capo Press paperback edition, 1985.

Ryan, Kathleen; Oestreich, Daniel; and Orr, George. *The Courageous Messenger*. Jossey-Bass, 1996.

Scott, Susan. *Fierce Conversations*. Viking Books, 2002.

Short, James F., Jr. "Social Organization and Risk: Some Current Controversies". *Annual Review of Sociology*. January 1, 1993.

Smith, Rebecca. and Emshwiller, John. *24 Days*. Harper Business, 2003.

Stone, Doug; Patton, Bruce; and Heen, Sheila. *Difficult Conversations*. Penguin Books, 1999.

Swartz, Mimi. and Watkins, Sherron. *Power Failure*. Doubleday, 2003.

Vaughan, Diane. *The Challenger Launch Decision*. The University of Chicago Press, 1996.

Resources

Webster's 7th Collegiate Dictionary, 1973.

Webster's New Unabridged Dictionary, 2003.

Weick, Karl. *Making Sense of the Organization*. Blackwell Publishing, 2001.

Weick, Karl. "Prepare Your Organization to Fight Fires". *Harvard Business Review*. May-June, 1996. Reprint 96311.

Weick, Karl. *Sensemaking in Organizations*. Sage, 1995.

Weick, Karl. *The Social Psychology of Organizing*. Random House, 1969, 1979.

Weick, Karl and Sutcliffe, Kathleen. *Managing the Unexpected*. Jossey-Bass, 2001.

Woods, David. *Beyond Human Error*. http://csel.eng.ohio-state.edu/woods.

Yamada, Ken. "Grove's Network Computer View". *Computer Reseller News*. October 28, 1996.

NOTES

NOTES